Communication

How To Communicate Effectively And Empathize With Others, As Well As Build Lasting Relationships Via Improved Social Skills And Self-assurance

(Learn More About The Benefits That Come From Communicating With Emotional Intelligence)

Jean-Pierre Hill

TABLE OF CONTENT

Introduction 1

Eye Contact 27

The Art Of Communicating Through Writing . 42

Take A Good Look At Your Achievements 66

In Order To Maintain An Image Of Expertise In The Workplace, Here Are Some Body Language Tips You May Use. 74

Culture - What Makes Us All The Same While Still Making Us Unique 83

How To Get Rid Of Your Obsessive Compulsive Disorder With Eye Contact Staring? 97

Educate Staff About The Key Performance Indicators Of The Company. 113

Charmingly Cool Charismatic 118

Sharing Information Within The Community 131

Making A Case For Yourself In The Working Environment 142

How To Have Profitable And Enjoyable Conversations And Why You Should 160

Introduction

The term "empathy" is one that is used rather often. Empathy is a trait that is widely acknowledged to be desirable; nonetheless, it is not always accorded the utmost significance in the lives of individuals.

Did you know that 98% of people are capable of sensing the emotions that other people are experiencing? The rare exceptions to this rule include those who suffer from psychopathy, narcissism, or sociopathy; these types of people are unable to grasp or respond to the thoughts and feelings of other people.

Another category of people who could have difficulty understanding the emotions of others is those who fall somewhere on the autistic spectrum. Many individuals think that persons who fall somewhere on the autistic spectrum are nevertheless able to empathize with the experiences of others, even if it's not in the same way that we typically understand empathy.

Even though the overwhelming majority of individuals have the capacity for empathy, the frequency with which they demonstrate it might vary greatly. But what precisely is meant by the term "empathy," and why is it so important?

In the first chapter, I discussed having empathy for others and having a good knowledge of them. The ability to see the world through the eyes of another person is called intercultural competence. It makes it easier for us to convey our ideas to other people in a manner that is comprehensible to them, which is essential to the process of establishing healthy social ties.

The second chapter then went on to examine how empathy may be utilized to strengthen and enhance communication, as well as shed some light on the reasons why this is such a crucial communication component.

In the third part of this article, I covered the many situations and contexts in which it is important for us to utilize and demonstrate empathy.

It is also crucial for readers to pay close attention to the fourth chapter, which encourages readers to cultivate empathy in their daily lives as an essential component of effective communication and satisfying interpersonal interactions. In this section, I focused more on the reasons why and the ways in which empathy is necessary to form powerful and enduring relationships.

Then, in the fifth section, I dedicated this chapter to outlining why empathy is required for the workplace and how to develop interpersonal understanding skills, especially in organizations to continually strive toward attaining the goals of the latter. Specifically, I focused on how to increase the ability to empathize with others in the workplace and how to enhance interpersonal understanding abilities. This is very necessary for the development of collaboration and teamwork.

I wrapped off the book by discussing how the concept of empathy might be applied to the many fields that deal with health and social care in chapter 6. This is an essential need that must be met before a health professional may achieve success. We would investigate how it affects the overall health of the patient as well as the health of the medical team.

So, does everyone naturally possess a certain amount of empathy, or is it something that can be taught? Are there certain people who simply have a more sensitive character by default? Is developing empathy really as important as some people make it out to be?

In this book, I made it a point to define empathy in connection to the context, location, and subject matter that would be discussed in each chapter. This is an important aspect of the book that I wanted to make sure to include.

Let us begin right now.

Competencies in Non-Verbal Communication

It is extremely simple to ignore non-verbal signals, despite the fact that they are an essential part of effective interpersonal communication. When they are not controlled properly, unintended non-verbal cues may communicate messages that are not clear and can even lead to misunderstandings.

1. Making Eye Contact and Expressing Yourself Through Your Face

Eye contact should be maintained at all times, and a cheerful look should be worn whenever possible to send the message that you are open to discussion. Maintain eye contact and be conscious of your facial expression at all times, regardless of how you're feeling. You really have to keep an eye out for these non-verbal signs if you want to improve your communication skills.

2. Body Language Nonverbal cues may convey a great deal of information. Take note of how you stand, sit, move, and hold your head while you do these things. Subtle gestures, posture, and stance may give out a lot of misleading messages to others. Your words might be expressing one thing while your body is suggesting something another. In order to prevent misunderstandings in the workplace, it is essential to pay attention to the nonverbal clues that are present.

Capabilities in Written Communication

In order for managers to do their jobs effectively, they need to be able to communicate well in writing as well. Because writing is the medium via which information is communicated both within and outside of any company, the quality of a professional manager's written communication will have a significant bearing on his career and the organization he manages. The following are some fundamental pointers to help you enhance your writing skills:

1. Be familiar with your goals.

You have to settle on your objectives before you can start putting your ideas down on paper. When you are attempting to get your point across to others, setting a particular goal can help you be more succinct and direct in your communication. When establishing your objectives, it is essential to take into account your target demographic; specifically, you should be aware of what they currently know, what they need knowledge of, and what you want to teach them.

2. Presentation and Organization

In the drafting of business or corporate papers, you are not required to use flowery language or analogies that are difficult to comprehend. Writing at the workplace need to be done with the intention of transmitting and spreading knowledge; hence, the structure ought to be centered on making the document understandable and well-organized. For instance, try beginning paragraphs with the major theme, and then following the main topic with extra explanation or a comparison. Another option is to attempt beginning paragraphs with supporting details.

3. The Draft, the Review, and the Edit

After you have determined your goals, found out who your audience is, and crafted your message in a way that is structured, the next step is to read it over again, make any necessary edits, and check to see whether all of your points were well communicated. Never send out a document without first doing a thorough proofreading — there are very few things that seem more unprofessional than a document that is riddled with mistakes.

May I Please Move?

You are free to go around. Movement is beneficial; it injects energy into a situation, but only if it gives the impression that it serves a purpose and that it was performed on purpose. You may, for instance, go to the other side of the space where the presentation is taking place. You don't need to worry about walking in front of any of the slides since they are of very little importance to you. Please don't worry about it. You have the option of moving forward one step or many steps to the side. Everything is feasible so long as it seems natural and you don't repeat yourself too often; in fact, it could even provide a wonderful touch of emphasis to whatever you are saying.

However, there are several issues that often arise with mobility, and you will need to take precautions to prevent them.

Movement is not something that should ever be "choreographed" in preparation or prepared at a certain moment in your presentation; for instance, in an attempt to stress a given topic. It will never seem natural, and it will be distracting to the experience. A scripted action will be evident and blatant, and it will interfere with both the rhythm and the meaning of the words. As a consequence of this, the audience will get distracted by the movement and will no longer pay attention to what you are saying.

You need to put forth a lot of effort to keep from "fidgeting." Movement that is distracting and makes you seem uncomfortable with what you are saying should be avoided at all costs. For instance, "hopping" from one foot to the other is a typical fidget that, as a matter of fact, is rather often triggered by standing with your weight more heavily distributed on one foot than the other. You switch to the other foot once one of your hips becomes fatigued, and then switch back until the other hip tires. You have undoubtedly seen speakers walking back and forth as they are giving presentations as well. A painfully prevalent behavior that is both a distracting "fidget" and a destroyer of eye contact is turning back and forth to slides too often and needlessly. This is a behavior that is tragically common.

Therefore, fidgeting is not only incredibly distracting but also fails to leave a powerful impression. How do you put a stop to it? Flop! Be careful to relax your muscles before you give your presentation, and focus on your breathing so that you can remain calm and focused while you speak.

Being seated Well

How can you express the power and assurance that you feel right now? The first step is to accept the fact that you will have to do more effort. And the reason I say this is because a lot of individuals have told me that they choose sitting since it is simpler and less intimidating than standing. I'll allow you that it could seem less intimidating, but in reality, it's far simpler to have presence and to command attention when you stand up. This is because your complete body is able to communicate a powerful impression and release the right amount of energy when you do so. When you take a seat, the table will obscure your view.

The secret is to first perfect a self-assured and balanced posture while standing, and then "swap" your secure and confident posture from the waist down for a chair. Once you have mastered this, the next step is to sit down. Make sure that your bottom is resting on the back of the chair, and that your feet are resting on the floor with a little bit of space between them. Then, in order to keep up the appearance of being poised, attentive, and ready, tilt your upper body ever-so-slightly forward and raise from the crown of your head. You are going to have to put in additional effort now, and make sure that you keep up your energy levels if you want to beat the table that is in front of you. Your facial expression, gesture, eye contact, and all the other positive things that we are going to speak about in a moment need to be functioning, working well, and just a little bit more than they need to in order for you to look calm and collected while you are standing up. It is obvious that you do not want to appear unduly energetic and frantic.

I want to emphasize once again that you are not required to always sit in this fashion. It is your location in the center. You are free to lean in whatever direction seems most comfortable to you—backwards, forwards, onto one arm or your elbows, cross your legs for a minute, etc. However, it can't be forced in any manner, shape, or form; it must occur organically. Your actions shouldn't devolve into distracting fidgeting either!

Speak without mumbling.

In communication, your enunciation, the loudness of your voice, and how you shout out the words are all extremely significant factors to consider. Check to see that the volume is just right, balancing neither too loud nor too mild. Additionally, pay attention to how you pronounce each word. Be careful that you pronounciate the words accurately since it is quite distracting to listen to someone who has the improper pronunciation of words. When you speak clearly, you will not only be able to convey your message to your audience but also explain to them what it is that you are attempting to communicate.

Try to refrain from stating the obvious.

Try to avoid asking questions that have answers that are too clear as much as you possibly can. You may keep your audience interested by asking thought-provoking questions that will get them thinking.

Consider Who You're Speaking To.

If you are going to talk, you should consider your audience and what they may take away from what you say. Think about how they will respond to what you are going to say and what emotions it will elicit in them. Because of this, if you want to make a sale to a consumer, you need to take into consideration the requirements that they have. Always try to put yourself in their position so that you may devise a statement that is certain to strike a chord with them. Always go out of your way to make your consumers feel valued. If you want to sell more of your product, use a tag line that speaks to the challenges that customers face and the requirements they have.

CARD OF THE HIEROPHANT IN THE TAROT

The Hierophant tarot card represents dedication to a cause. When the Hierophant appears in a tarot reading for you about your twin flame, it indicates that there is consistency in your feeling of safety towards your upcoming reunion as well as in your life in general. If you are enquiring about the possibility of reuniting with your twin flame, the Hierophant suggests making a commitment that will allow you to feel safe. The hierophant represents the kind of connection in which both partners enter the partnership with the intention of learning more about themselves in the process. They have the potential to grow so reliant on one another that they don't even know how to function in the world without the other.

Getting the Hierophant as a love omen, particularly if you are hoping for a committed relationship with your twin flame, is a very positive sign indeed.

The Hierophant gives you indications and a feeling of safety, which enables you to pursue the things in life that you have always sought.

You will experience progress on both a spiritual and a material level when you are in partnership with your twin flame.

In contrast to the Emperor connection, the Hierophant relationship is characterized by ease. This is particularly true when compared to the Emperor relationship.

The Hierophant is a symbol for two independent people of equal standing who achieve achievement together. The Hierophant is often a symbol for two persons, one of whom is acting as a teacher or mentor to the other, and both of whom are deeply committed to disseminating their knowledge to others. You and your twin flame are two individuals who have a unique connection with one another owing to the fact that you both have the same soul mission.

You will both inspire and motivate one another, and you will often find themselves traveling together. You will also frequently maintain a very youthful spirit, constantly seeking for a new adventure that you can share with one another.

The Hierophant mentions a form of 21 that does not put up opposition.

a connection that allows you to unwind and chill off. Because you have the same kinds of views and ideals, you don't have to try as hard to impress one another because you already do it naturally. You are successful even when you are not making any effort at all. Both of you can't even fathom what life would be like without the other, and your twin flame can't even fathom what life would be like without you. You are both on the same level, and in addition to being a love pair, you are also each other's closest friend.

When there is going to be a wedding in the near future, a reading will often call attention to the Hierophant. In the event that you are seeking guidance on your connection with your twin flame, the Hierophant indicates that it is safe and sound.

You and your twin flame will spend most of your time together traveling, instructing, learning, and sharing experiences that are significant to both of you. It is in both of your best interests to pursue a goal in tandem. Because neither of you wants to be with anyone else except the other, this kind of relationship almost often ends up being one that is fought against all odds.

Cues that are not Verbal

It is common knowledge that communication involves a great deal more than simply the exchange of words. There is also something known as body language, which may be characterized by clues such as a person's posture, facial expressions, eye contact, and gestures. It has come to our attention that the way in which we understand what another person is saying may be significantly influenced by non-verbal clues. For instance, if someone is looking away from you and down while they are talking to you, it may give the impression that they cannot be trusted. On the other hand, if they keep eye contact with you and have an open posture, you could take them more seriously as a source of information. In addition, some facial expressions are capable of communicating meaning even when words alone are not being used. For example, a raised eyebrow might be interpreted as a sign of suspicion or incredulity.

1. The Language of the Body

What we really say might be heavily influenced by how we present ourselves physically. For instance, if we are seated with our arms firmly crossed over our chests, we are likely to give the impression that we are disagreeable and defensive. On the other side, if we sit in a manner that is open and inviting to others, we increase the likelihood that they will find us accessible and trustworthy. The way that we hear people might also be affected by their body language. For example, if someone is looking straight at us and speaking in a voice that is easy to understand, we are more likely to pay attention to what they are saying and comprehend what they are saying. However, we are less likely to absorb what someone is saying if they are muttering or diverting their eyes when they are speaking to us. When we are gathered in a circle and a new person approaches us with the intention of joining the discussion, the first thing that we do to let them know whether or not they are welcome is communicate with them through our body language. Either we acknowledge their existence and open our body language to them, or we choose to ignore them and maintain a closed posture. When you are next in a discussion, pay attention to your body language and analyze how it influences the message that you are conveying to the other person.

2. Tone

Everyone has their own distinctive manner of speech, and the circumstances or setting almost always play a significant role in shaping that manner. For instance, you probably won't use the same tone of voice while speaking to your closest friend as you do when speaking to your employer. Your current state of mind may also have an effect on the quality of your voice; for example, when you are pleased, you may talk with a higher pitch, but when you are furious, you may speak with a lower pitch and a harsher tone. Additionally, the way in which you deliver your message might communicate vital information to the listener. For instance, your tone of voice will change depending on whether you are providing someone with instructions or relating the events of your day to them. Therefore, the manner in which you deliver your message may have a big influence on how it is understood by the recipient.

3. Placing an emphasis on

When we emphasize anything, we are giving certain words or phrases an increased amount of weight. This may be done for a number of different reasons, but the most common ones are to communicate strong feelings or to make a point in a more concise manner. The meaning of what we are saying may also be altered by the way that we emphasize certain words or phrases. Therefore, highlighting certain parts of a book may be an effective technique for both public presenters and authors. It has the potential to assist bring emphasis and clarity to our message if it is used appropriately. However, it is also possible to abuse it, which may lead to misunderstanding or even the wrong impression being drawn. As a result, it is essential to exercise caution about the things that you highlight and the tone in which you do so.

The use of emphasis helps to convey feeling. When you tell a tale, putting more emphasis on specific aspects of the narrative helps portray a more complete image. When you're in an angry state, the way you emphasize words might come out as aggressive. The use of emphasis is a potent means of communicating beyond only the words that we are speaking; it lends additional significance to those words.

Eye Contact

When you gaze into the eyes of another person, what do you see? In my view, you are able to provide a great deal of information. how a person is now feeling. what kind of feelings they have for you. What it is that they desire. Additionally, it conveys to the recipient that you are paying them your whole attention. When someone is speaking to you, making eye contact with them and looking them in the eyes to demonstrate that you are paying attention to what they are saying is a respectful gesture.

Making and maintaining eye contact may be challenging at times. Eye contact is something that is lot more natural for women than it is for males. If you are out on a date with a lady and you don't make any eye contact with her, there is a good possibility that you won't be asked out on a second date. The fact of the matter is that everyone can improve their ability to maintain eye contact. Making eye contact is a talent, and I'll demonstrate how you may improve your ability to do it in this lesson.

It is possible to convey a great deal about yourself just by avoiding establishing eye contact. Now, of course, if this is something that is important to the culture, you shouldn't worry about it. You may ignore the information in this chapter if, in the society in which you were raised, making eye contact is considered impolite or is not the norm. In the culture of the United States, eye contact is very important. It demonstrates that you have confidence, which makes you more appealing, which makes you more trustworthy, and which helps others regard you as warm and friendly.

Maintaining healthy eye contact conveys a number of important messages about both you as a person and the others with whom you are conversing. Making eye contact with the person you are speaking with, whether it be your employer, a friend, a member of your family, or a colleague, conveys to that person that you respect and understand them.

When I was working in Antarctica, I recall going to a pub with several of my friends and seeing a stunning woman wearing a red dress. She was seated at the bar. My attention was immediately pulled to her as she walked from person to person, smiling and making small talk with each one. I couldn't help but grin the moment her eyes locked with mine for the first time. To make a long story short, I ended up marrying that girl. The eyes convey attention even without a spoken word being spoken between the parties, which is a potent kind of communication.

Simply giving someone your whole attention might elicit a sense of gratitude. Those of you who are reading this who are parents already know this. When they are fed, cuddled, and soothed, newborn newborns express love and thanks in their own unique ways. They do not express their gratitude verbally but rather via the expressions on their faces. The love and admiration that they have for you is palpable in the way that they look at you. Even if they are unable to communicate verbally, they nonetheless find a way to show you how much love they have for you.

Have you ever been in a situation when you could tell someone all you wanted to say with only a look? If yes, describe the setting. This gaze tells the other that you comprehend what they are saying. When someone says something idiotic at work and you look over at a colleague and see that they are nodding their head in agreement with what the idiot said. Or when you do something that your wife does not approve of and you can tell simply by the look she gives you that you have made a mistake in what you did. There are many more instances of this that I could provide.

The Link Between Autism and Eye Contact

Making eye contact with someone else may be a very stressful experience for some people. People who have autism have an exceptionally high incidence of this problem. Because autism is growing more widespread in the United States, I believe it is important to bring up this topic and explore whether or not eye contact should be required.

When talking to someone who has autism, just because they avoid making eye contact does not indicate that they are not paying attention to what you are saying. This almost always indicates that the person is uncomfortable or suffers from a significant amount of anxiety. Regrettably, this may lead to wrong perceptions or assumptions, particularly in the American society, where maintaining eye contact is thought to be of utmost importance.

If your kid has a handicap and there is anything in this book that makes them feel uneasy, you should probably steer clear of it. Getting pleasure and avoiding suffering are the two primary goals in life. If making eye contact causes you or your kid distress or anguish, please do not make them go through this exercise; instead, continue forward to the next step. This book has a variety of different tasks that readers may perform to develop their communication skills in various areas.

Rules

The guidelines for maintaining eye contact are easy to understand but might shift depending on the context. It is important to me that the ideas presented here be understood by everyone. The standard recommendation is to maintain eye contact for a couple of seconds. If you have three to five seconds, glance to the side, and then look back. In addition to this, it is essential to focus on one eye at a time. Break eye contact and shift your focus to the right eye after looking at the left eye for a few seconds at the beginning of the exercise. This guideline is applicable to everyday discourse now.

For example, with a close friend or member of the family.

The time requirements for groups are the same. Be careful to give each individual in the group the same amount of time as you examine their eyes when you are working with the group. Like three seconds from person to person, and continue doing this until you've gone through everyone in the group. This demonstrates that you are paying attention and actively talking with each individual to ensure that nobody feels excluded from the conversation.

When it comes to dating, maintaining eye contact is important. Now, when you're out on a date with someone, you shouldn't simply stare them down without blinking or making any other facial gestures. Maintain your lively demeanor, but make an effort to gaze at the person you're out with for a longer period of time. Doing so will showcase your self-assurance and make you seem more appealing to others.

The same criteria apply while you're at work: give each person you're talking to three to five seconds of your full attention, and attempt to maintain eye contact with them throughout the conversation. When you talk during meetings, you should strive to establish eye contact with everyone in the room. Everyone who is there at the meeting will have the impression that they are contributing.

Speaking in front of an audience is like confronting an animal, and most individuals are scared of it. Performing in front of an audience is a challenge in and of itself, but you also need to keep them interested and delighted. Your ability to create eye contact and connect with the people in the audience may often make the difference between having an audience that is bored and one that is interested. Make an effort to include each and every person. Make direct eye contact with a few individuals at random across the throng. If you find that establishing direct eye contact with them makes you feel uneasy, try looking towards the tops of their heads instead. If you are at a sufficient distance from them, they won't be able to tell whether or not you are establishing eye contact with them.

Workout number 3.1

Depending on how comfortable you are initiating eye contact, this exercise will have numerous phases for you to complete. Determine which one you are capable of managing, and then start there.

Option 1: Take a gander in the rearview mirror. Begin here if you do not feel ready to go out and make eye contact with anybody, even your friends and relatives. Timing is another skill that may be greatly improved by doing this. Take three to five seconds to concentrate on one eye before moving on to the other. When you are able to gaze into your own eyes, you have taken a significant step toward being able to see into the eyes of others.

Option 2: Connect to the internet. Today, there is a plethora of video content available on the internet that serves as an excellent tool for practicing eye contact. Watch eye contact videos, vlogs, or simply just search for them online. Watch the video in full screen mode, then keep working on this technique until you feel more at ease with it. Even doing something as simple as having a video conference with a friend might count as practice. Try skyping a member of your family and focusing on their eyes when they appear on the screen. It won't be as taxing as making eye contact with someone in person, and it will be excellent practice.

Option 3: Practicing with a buddy is highly recommended. Make direct eye contact with a friend or another person with whom you feel at ease while you are seated face to face with them. You have the option of beginning with a little period of time and gradually increasing it as you get more comfortable, or you may make an effort to maintain eye contact for the longest possible period of time.

Option 4: During conversations, try establishing more eye contact with others. Be sure to stick to the guidelines laid forth above, and give this as much practice as you can. Especially when dealing with individuals who have the potential to intimidate you, such as a boss or someone to whom you are attracted. This will demonstrate that you are developing confidence and may cause a shift in how they see you in their minds.

Workout number 3.2

Perform this exercise after you have reached a point where you are confident in all of the aforementioned areas. You are now required to establish eye contact with everyone you greet as you pass them on the street. Even if it's not very long, you're going to find yourself establishing eye contact with a lot of individuals you don't even know. Consider each passing gaze to be a new, though brief, point of contact that you have established. If you want to get some bonus points for this activity, try to recall the eye colors of the persons you greet when you see them in the future. You should decide on a number that you are at ease with and do your best to remember it. This will not only cause you to glance at the eyes, but it will also cause you to pay a heightened level of attention to them.

I really hope you liked this chapter, and that it has opened your eyes to the importance of maintaining healthy eye contact. The more often you do these exercises, the more at ease you will become creating eye contact regardless of the setting you find yourself in. In the next chapter, I will discuss the practice of active listening and the reasons why it is necessary for effective communication. Listen to what I have to say, and I assure you that you won't regret it.

An Appeal to Take Action

One other negative pattern of behavior is one that involves poor listening skills.

You end up reacting to a trigger with the proper poor listening habits, which hinder you from truly digesting the content that is being sent to you. This indicates that in order to improve your poor listening abilities, you will need to use the same strategy that is used in order to break undesirable habits. As a result, the identical call to action that was in the prior chapter will be included in this one, but with a few modifications.

Keep an Eye on Your Unhealthy Listening Habits.

Find a habit tracker app that works for you by going to the app store on your own device, then searching for one there. You also have the option of keeping a manual journal, which you may do either on your own personal device or on a paper notebook.

When you next engage in a behavior that irritates you, make a note of it in either the diary that you keep or the mobile app of your choosing. Be careful to describe the specifics of the habit loop, which include the trigger, the behavior, and the reward. Keep a record of these particulars for each occurrence that takes place. In due time, you will see that there is a pattern developing. You have become aware that you have a terrible habit of listening at this stage.

It's time to break some bad listening habits and get back on track.

After you have recognized a bad listening behavior, you will need to break the tendency in order to improve your listening skills. You should write down the replacement behavior that you want to adopt (such as removing distractions, participating in the discussion, or checking the accuracy of what you believe you heard) as well as how you intend to reward yourself for adopting the new behavior. When the trigger event happens, the new behavior should be applied, along with the updated reward. Keep in mind that if you don't give yourself a reward, it will be far more difficult for a new habit to persist.

Maintain a record of both the previous and the current behavior. If you are able to maintain consistency and have adequate patience. You will see that the old habit becomes less prevalent over time, while the new conduct becomes more prevalent. You will improve your ability to listen to others to the degree that you are able to rid yourself of inadequate listening skills and continue to replace them with abilities that require active participation.

The Art Of Communicating Through Writing

Written communications are far more challenging than spoken communications, even over the phone, especially when compared to face-to-face interactions. When you communicate anything in writing, you truly put your communication abilities to the test. To effectively deliver a message in a way that is understandable and has the appropriate tone, you need to learn how to become a wordsmith of the greatest regard.

When someone is reading your words on a screen, they cannot determine your disposition based on your body language or your tone of voice. Because each side of the discussion is taking place in isolation, it is hard to demonstrate that you comprehend what is being said by active listening even though the dialogue is not one-sided. To effectively explain what you want to say, you have to focus nearly entirely on the choice of words you use.

When people communicate by texting or email, they often fail to fully get one another's meaning. This is due to the fact that the meaning might be lost if the appropriate words are not selected. It is possible that you may come out sounding as if you are furious when, in reality, all you are trying to do is be succinct. It is difficult to strike this precise balance without prior experience since it requires a lot of concentration.

The Three Characteristics of Communicating through Writing

It should come as no surprise that the majority of the four characteristics of successful communication that were just reviewed do not apply to written communications. Instead, we are going to make some adjustments to this in order to better accommodate written communications. Word choice, tone, and acknowledgement are going to be the focus of the investigation.

Choice of Words

When it comes to drafting email messages, you have to be extremely selective with the words that you use. You may not have the option to clear up any misconceptions, in contrast to when you are communicating with someone personally. It is preferable to avoid employing slang, idioms, and metaphorical language and instead make use of straightforward language that is easy to comprehend.

When you are communicating with another person through text, you should avoid using any acronyms unless you are positive that they are familiar with them. You do not want the word's meaning to be thrown off just because you did not write it completely. Always err on the side of caution; it is the wisest course of action. If you are texting a person who is close to you, such as your spouse, a close friend, a parent, or a kid, it is likely that you are familiar with the person's messaging style and the acronyms that they are familiar with. If you are messaging someone that you do not know very well, it is in your best interest to avoid talking to them at all costs.

Tone

When we write communications, the majority of the time we are reading it back to ourselves in our own voice and in the manner in which we would talk if we were having the conversation in person. On the other hand, the receiver of that communication could interpret it in a different manner entirely. Because they are unable to hear the inflection in your speech, this information must be communicated in another manner.

Sentence structure is the most effective method for establishing the mood of a communication delivered through email. A tone of impatience, dissatisfaction, or rage might be communicated by a sequence of extremely short and very succinct phrases. Multiple lengthy sentences or paragraphs could be able to express a more conversational or pleasant tone, but they might also contribute to an unneeded lengthening of the whole text.

Utilizing a variety of sentence lengths, including both long and short ones, and grouping them into concise paragraphs that are simple to understand is the most effective strategy to convey a non-confrontational attitude in your written electronic interactions. This strategy provides a neutral backdrop for your message, which will enable the reader to concentrate on the literal meaning of the words rather than speculating about the probable intentions that were being sent by those words.

When communicating through text, it is essential to bear in mind that the other party is unable to discern the tone of voice that you would be using if you were speaking to them in person. They are unable to perceive the state of your emotions. It's possible that you're saying something in jest, but the other person could take it seriously since they don't realize you're joking around if you say anything to them. It is also crucial that you do not make any jokes or idle comments that might be interpreted in an unpleasant manner. A sentence may be interpreted in a manner that is not intended, which may be the source of many disagreements in personal relationships.

Recognition and thanks

Even if you are not actively listening to what is being said to you, it is essential that you recognize any prior messages or discussions that led up to the textual communication you are producing. In addition to letting the recipient know that you have in fact read all of their prior messages, this kind of acknowledgement places the email message being read into its proper perspective for the recipient.

When you text, you may also utilize the acknowledgement function. If you get a text message from someone requesting you to go to the shop, for instance, you may react by saying that you would gladly pick up the item in question from the business in question. This ensures that everyone is on the same page and that they are aware that you have truly read the material that they have provided.

Why Communicate?

It is a crucial talent for everyday life to be able to communicate one's thoughts, ideas, and facts to another person. to comprehend other people while also being understood oneself. We communicate for a number of different purposes, including to provide information, to answer questions, to make observations, to forge connections, to provide comments, to cultivate relationships, to evaluate, and to start social dialogues. There is no limit to the possible explanations. Without connection, we would continue to live on our own separate islands, cut off from any possibility of holistic advancement.

To be a Good Communicator: You Will Use the Tool of Communication to Transfer Ideas "Effectively" and "Efficiently" We may assist ourselves and the person take the next step by using instruments of communication, which also allow us to affect changes in the attitudes and behaviors of both ourselves and other people. Maintain everyone's sense of drive.

What exactly do we mean when we talk about communication?

The act of sending information from at least one person to another individual or group is what we mean when we talk about communication. It is comprised of three essential components: the sender, the receiver, and the message itself. In order for there to be communication, the message must first make its way via any channel of communication and then be received by the intended receiver. A chat face-to-face, an audio call, a video call, an email, a letter, a note, a text message, a formal proposal, and/or a video conference might be among the modes of communication.

If you want to be a good communicator, you will look out for context, culture, emotional wellness, and mutually understood language. This will guarantee that the message is received with the same relevance and effect as it was intended. Therefore, the message sent by the sender should, in an ideal world, have the same meaning for the receiver. The sender has the burden of being able to encode words, ideas, feelings, sensations, and needs, as well as information, in such a manner that it may be properly ingested by the recipient.

What is the key distinction between just talking and really communicating?

Talking is nothing more than the intentional utterance of words with the goal of communicating something to another person. It depends on how well you do the activity. On the other hand, communication is light years ahead, since it guarantees that the message is effectively transported to its destination. It's a talent that's worth acquiring and honing to your full potential.

To Have Effective Communication Skills: You have to educate yourself on how to take your thoughts and actions out of the "auto-pilot" mode and into the "strategic" mode by making effective use of various communication tools. After that, you'll go from being a thoughtless talker to an adept communicator, which is a huge step forward.

You will be able to convey your most valuable ideas, abilities, and inputs in an effective manner with no loss of transmission, and you will also have the ability to understand the replies to those questions. After completing this whole cycle of talking and listening, you will be consciously prepared to take action ahead of time and get closer to the goal that you have set for yourself. There is no such thing as an effective leader who is not also an effective communicator.

Why do we continue to sprinkle our articles and motivational presentations with quotations from people like Gandhi, Swami Vivekananda, Field Marshall Manekshaw, Subhash Chandra Bose, and Winston Churchill? Because there is no question that, in addition to being fantastic leaders, they were also astounding orators!

How to go from being someone who rambles on without thinking to becoming someone who can effectively communicate with others

What are the origins of the term "skill"?

"The ability to perform an action with a goal in mind in a given amount of time or energy or both is considered to be a skill. This ability must be learned." Generally speaking, skills may be broken down into two categories: domain-general skills and domain-specific skills.

Therefore, communication is a talent that can be learnt, and if it is performed carefully and intentionally, it will get you closer to the goal that you have set for yourself. Talking without any focus or organization is a waste of time that does not stimulate the intellect. It is of no assistance to either the one doing the talking/sending or the person doing the receiving in terms of moving on to the next stage or really taking action.

Communication exists in both the general and the domain-specific realms; the former is when it is utilized in everyday casual conversation, while the latter is when it is used as a tool or an arrow to strike the target and complete the task at hand. This is particularly obvious in workplaces because of the emphasis placed on objectives and bottom lines in such settings.

You will need to be able to effectively communicate in order to send and receive information if you want to be a good communicator. If you use them on a regular basis, having strong communication skills will provide you the ability to communicate in a way that is clear, effective, and efficient. In order to accomplish our goal in the job as well as in other social circumstances, we first need to acquire this talent and then polish it via practice.

What does it mean when it's referred to as a "critical skill"?

The ability to communicate effectively is a crucial and strategic talent that is very vital for one's success in the profession. Due to the fact that it has the potential to make or break a transaction, it cannot be considered only a soft talent. Therefore, if you want to succeed in life, business, and leadership, you need to have excellent skills in mindful communication.

If you want to be an effective communicator, your communication skills at work need to do three things: increase productivity, raise optimism, and allow capabilities for both you and others around you.

Is it possible to teach oneself?

You can, in fact, educate yourself on the concepts of excellent and successful communication; you can then imbibe them, practice them, and seek feedback to monitor your development on this essential talent. Take a test to determine your current level of communication expertise, make a note of the areas in which you are deficient, and then make a conscious effort to incorporate the suggested strategies into your regular conversations in order to strengthen the areas in which you are weakest.

If you want to be a good communicator, you could find it beneficial to employ a strategy that is focused on action and is called Start, Continue, and Stop. This is particularly helpful after receiving feedback since it allows you to begin a few new things, continue a few things that you have found to be doing well, and stop some things that you have found to be getting in the way of successful communication. When you combine strategies like these with attentive application, not only will you become a better and more rapid learner, but you will also become an expert in the practice of effective communication skills.

Is it freeing or does it place restrictions?

Knowledge is a discipline that can set you free, and communication is one of those disciplines. Once you have gained an understanding of and mastered the skill set necessary for successful communication, you will be able to determine which tools have the potential to function in any given circumstance and use those tools in the appropriate manner. Your ability to communicate effectively may get you to a place where you can achieve the results you want in a given circumstance if you continue to hone your abilities through practice. Therefore, communication is seen as the key to success in the job as well as in life in general, according to these people. You are engaging with people on actual ground, which brings you closer together, and you are aligning your purpose and objective on a shared level, both of which are liberating experiences.

You need to be aware of the fact that communication is a skillful combination of science and art in order to be an effective communicator. Similar to the scientific method, communication is a body of information that includes rules, theories, and facts. It is also an Art, since the individualized application and creativeness with which it is used in a given circumstance will reveal its final effectiveness in that circumstance. They think that communication may be effective for those who put effort into it.

It is freeing because you realize that some kind of communication will absolutely function even in the most difficult of circumstances, given that you comprehend it. People that are successful are adept at communicating in order to achieve their goals. In addition, other advantages, such as inclusion, creativity, clarity, purpose, and pleasure, are produced as a side effect.

The ability to communicate effectively is directly related to increased personal development and empowerment. It helps one become a more powerful leader, a more productive team member, and an overall more effective person overall.

It is always a good idea, after an organization has made the choice to look at an external agency for assistance with PR, to first list out the comparative capabilities of a minimum of five different agencies, and then to pick a few of those agencies so that they can be asked for a capability presentation. after the business has made this decision, it is always a good idea.

After the invitations to the agency pitches have been sent out, the person in the organization who is in charge of public relations or marketing and is driving the efforts forward must also ensure that there is broader engagement from the top leadership at the actual time of the agency pitches that have been chosen.

It is a common practice in many businesses to skip over this essential step in the process of making decisions concerning public relations (PR). This may be due to a lack of time, or it may be due to a lack of understanding on how important it is to get a diverse perspective on what is on offer in terms of a strategy and execution plan, how the company will benefit in general, and how it is important for all to work in sync, in order to achieve the PR plan, and the overall marketing plan.

Also, if there were simply PR in the discussion thread, it would imply that following the pitch, the team would be required to record some of the specifics, the deliverables, and the commercials for internal consumption. This would either result in redundant effort or the production of work that might have been avoided.

When a larger internal audience participates directly in the stage of the pitch, there is sufficient space for required and relevant talks, which might cover a much broader gamut than what simply the public relations or marketing team would have with the agency. This makes it possible for the company to make better decisions. This results in involvement in the full meaning of the word right from the beginning phases of the process, which ultimately leads to a reasonable degree of engagement on the part of the relevant stakeholders in the organization.

Having such a broad participation and subsequent engagement in the current PR planning and execution also means that there is a feeling of belonging and buy-in in whatever is being planned, conceptually developed, and put into action by the communications team and the PR firm. This is because having such a broad participation and consequent engagement in the ongoing PR planning and execution leads to greater engagement.

More significantly, when everyone is aware of what is going on in the realm of reputation management, the group has a far greater inclination to celebrate successes and reflect on failures, which is a significant improvement. It is much simpler to get a hand and view of all those engaged, and there is a feeling of understanding on the how and why of PR, from the viewpoint of the broader organization. When there are problems that need to be handled, any course correction, or a relook in broad PR strategy, it is much easier to get a hand and view of those concerns.

Take A Good Look At Your Achievements

Your level of self-confidence will rise when you are able to state things like, "I can do this, and here is how I know this to be true." As part of your examination, you need to have uncovered the aspects of yourself that are particularly strong.

Make a record of your accomplishments and prioritize the top ten items on the list. Perhaps you earned a perfect score on the SATs, which is the best attainable score. Perhaps you earned the greatest possible score on the final exam. Perhaps you were successful in beating out the other candidates for the job advancement. It's possible that anything you did had a good influence on the lives of another person.

Take a look at all of your accomplishments and use them as a springboard for creating positive affirmations about the various qualities you possess. If you have the tendency of continuously weakening your confidence by talking poorly about yourself, affirmations may be quite effective in helping you break this behavior.

Prepare in advance how you will react.

Do you often respond with an affirmative answer without giving it much thought? If this is the case, you may find it helpful to have some standard responses prepared in advance for situations in which you are extended an invitation or made a request that you do not want to fulfill. Some examples of excellent ones are:

"There is a conflict in my schedule," you say.

"I need to take a look at my schedule."

"I'm afraid I won't be able to; I have other commitments."

"Allow me some time to research that and get back to you."

If you choose to respond by saying that you will check your schedule, you will be required to contact the individual again after you have "checked." It would be impolite for you not to do so. It is important to bear in mind that you are under no obligation to provide an explanation for declining an invitation or request.

You may practice being aggressive in a number of different ways, including coming up with words to say when you are offered an invitation or asked for something. Beginning practicing some common scenarios that you may face, particularly for circumstances in which you know you'll have a tougher time being forceful, is a good place to start if you want to improve your ability to be assertive. Repeat your answer out loud as you practice it. Before you get started with the practice, you may also find it helpful to sketch down a script. You should probably try role-playing with a trusted coworker or friend if you want to get the most out of the experience. They will then be able to provide you comments in this manner.

When you first begin putting your assertiveness abilities to use in the real world, start with low-risk circumstances. Try practicing assertive communication, for instance, with a close friend or spouse before moving on to more challenging and high-stakes scenarios at work. You should do a self-evaluation after every time you assert yourself to see whether or not you tackled the circumstance in a suitable way.

Talk to yourself in a positive way.

When you're in the thick of things, it may be incredibly challenging to put assertiveness skills to use. Because of this, it's a smart idea to give oneself a confidence boost by engaging in positive self-talk. Hyping yourself up with the reminders, "My time is important," or "I've got this," may really help you out if you're getting ready for a discussion in which you know you're going to have to put your foot down. This might seem corny, but if you're getting ready for a conversation in which you know you're going to have to put your foot down, hyping yourself up with the reminders can really help you out.

Because it may be either good or negative, the way in which we speak to ourselves can have a significant impact on both our level of self-assurance and our capacity to be forceful. Negative self-talk is harmful to us and leads us to assume that we are incapable of achieving certain goals. Our sense of self-worth, self-confidence, and self-respect all suffer as a result, which, of course, has a knock-on effect on our capacity to stand up for ourselves. The critical voice we hear in our heads is just as harmful as if it came from an actual bully.

On the other side, if you engage in positive self-talk, you will become more self-assured and confident as a result of this. Athletes often engage in self-talk that is upbeat and encouraging in the hopes that it would assist them in breaking past their own barriers and improving their capacity to handle discomfort. You could find it helpful to say positive affirmations to yourself on a daily basis and especially before engaging in potentially challenging talks. Affirmations have the power to alter how a person views himself, which is something that will surprise you. This change will be reflected in how you think about yourself going forward. In addition to this, it may help you find your voice and give you a greater sense of personal agency.

Develop a Sharp Perspective

It is essential to have a well-thought-out plan for your life if you want to realize your goals, achieve your desires, and do the work that brings you satisfaction. You must have a clear idea of what it is that you desire before you can be aggressive. One of the most important components of assertiveness is being aware of both the things that you are willing to do and the things that you are not willing to do in order to realize your goals. When it comes to deciding how successful you will be, both sides of the coin have the same amount of weight. Gaining clarity enables you to get rid of thoughts and actions that don't contribute anything of value to your goal. When you have a distinct plan in mind, you are better able to concentrate inward and draw from the resources, talents, and capabilities you possess in order to collaborate with others to go ahead.

A clear vision for your life may be created with the help of a few easy principles, which are as follows:

Make sure that everyone understands your vision. What exactly is it that you want to make happen in this life? Develop a strategy that looks far into the future.

Establish your objectives in detail. Develop a set of intermediate objectives that, when accomplished, will get you closer to achieving your long-term objective.

Imagine yourself succeeding, and train your mind to think positively. Think about the kind of person you want to be and the kind of communicator you want to be. Creating a good picture of yourself may help you reframe how you view yourself, which can contribute to increased levels of self-respect and self-confidence.

Put out the effort to improve yourself and expand your horizons. This is all about breaking out of your comfort zone and achieving success despite the difficulties and hurdles you face.

Pay attention to the qualities that you excel in. Learn to recognize your best qualities and capitalize on them.

In Order To Maintain An Image Of Expertise In The Workplace, Here Are Some Body Language Tips You May Use.

1. MAKE AN ATTEMPT TO AVOID RECLINING

When you lean back, it might indicate that you are fatigued or that you are done with the conversation. If you want to show that you are interested in something, lean back somewhat or at the very least sit up straight in your seat.

2. MAKE AN EFFORT TO AVOID FOLDING YOUR ARMS.

This indicator could provide the impression of defiance in the best case situation, in which it is turned off. People will believe that you are weird or impartial. They will accept this about you. You would not benefit in any way from any of the two hypotheses.

3. MAKE AN ATTEMPT TO KEEP YOUR EYE CONTACTS AND TRY NOT TO AVOID THEM.

People will automatically assume you have something to hide if you can't stare at them straight in the eye without flinching. Make every effort to avoid gaining a reputation for being difficult to understand or unreliable. Remember that making eye contact is a sign of trustworthiness in the business world.

4. MAKE EVERY ATTEMPT TO REDUCE YOUR GAZING

It is not impossible to establish a connection visually. This may come off as odd or even aggressive to certain people. Make an effort to reach a balance that is mutually acceptable and accommodating. Try your best not to make direct eye contact with anybody for more than three seconds at a time.

5. MAKE AN EFFORT TO AVOID GRIPPING YOUR HANDS

People who are forced to do things tend to. Whoever you are having a conversation with will notice the strain that you are under. Relax, and rest your hands in an open position next to you.

6. ATTEMPT NOT TO HIDE YOUR HANDS AS MUCH AS POSSIBLE.

It is possible that putting your hands behind your back or in your pockets is OK for you, but others have a tendency to interpret this as a hint that you are trying to hide anything from them.

7. MAKE EVERY ATTEMPT TO RESULTANT

Because you have something really important to say, you are gesturing quite firmly right now. You should make an effort to avoid slashing the air with your hands since this gives the impression that you are being cruel and arrogant to the person that you are speaking with.

8. MAKE EVERY ATTEMPT TO AVOID CONTACT WITH YOUR FACE

As with the previous point, this is another one that is often confused with a sign of dishonesty. It is in your best interest to avoid it.

9. MAKE AN ATTEMPT TO REDUCE THE VOLUME OF YOUR GESTURES

You're eager to impart some of your thoughtfulness and knowledge onto others, but there's a chance that you'll end up embarrassing someone instead. You can come out as weak and accommodating, or on the other hand, as apathetic to the situation.

10. MAKE EVERY ATTEMPT TO STAY STILL

It gives the impression that you are completely nuts, and it may also increase the level of worry experienced by the person who is watching you wriggle about. You might also give the impression of being too fatigued or nervous.

11. MAKE AN ATTEMPT TO RESTRAIN YOUR HUNCHBACK

You will act as if you are disheartened or sluggish or so exhausted that you cannot even imagine working normally. Put your shoulders back and put the focus on your face! It is not enough to rely just on your thinking to do the task.

12. MAKE SURE YOU DON'T MESS UP WHERE YOU'RE SITTING

It is the same as holding your hands together if you fold your feet or legs over the legs of your seat. You will come off as nervous and irritate the person with whom you are conversing.

13. MAKE AN ATTEMPT TO STOP MAKING YOURSELF SMALL

Make every effort not to flinch from the situation. It will give the impression that there is no certainty. Take a try at broadening areas where you may normally agree and see what kind of influence this might have on your business.

14. MAKE AN ATTEMPT TO AVOID GOING TOO BIG

Do everything it takes to keep from moving in such an uncontrollable manner or being so sweeping that it gives the impression that you are performing in front of an audience. This can have the opposite effect of what you want it to have. Additionally, it has the potential to terrify people.

15. AVOID POINTING YOUR FEET IN WEIRD DIRECTIONS AS MUCH AS POSSIBLE.

The fact that your feet are pointed in the wrong direction is something that a few people will notice, despite the fact that it can seem to be an odd thing to do.

16. MAKE AN ATTEMPT TO REFRAIN FROM GIVING YOURSELF COMPLIMENTS

Your colleagues and management will not find it encouraging if you pat your legs, regardless of whether you believe it is or not. They will just believe you to be completely uncomfortable, which will in turn cause them to behave awkwardly themselves.

17. MAKE AN ATTEMPT TO REFRAIN FROM CHECKING THE TIME (OR YOUR TELEPHONE!)

Just don't do it. It is beyond comprehension how impolite you can be. Maintain your focus on the conversation at hand, with the exception of necessary interruptions such as checking the clock or taking an important call.

18. AVOID MAKING CONTACT WITH OTHER PEOPLE BY USING THE POINT OF YOUR FINGER WHENEVER POSSIBLE.

If you are with someone at a point in your relationship when it is OK to fake trust or openness by contacting them rapidly, you should do it with the whole of your hand rather than the tip of your finger. You're not really E.T.

19. MAKE AN ATTEMPT TO IGNORe THE PROMPTS.

When you are unsure of what to say next, emulate the body language of your conversationalist. You are free to move in response to their signal. Do the same thing they are doing if you see them standing tall with an expectant expression on their face.

20. AVOID ATTACKING THE AIR POCKET IF YOU CAN.

When you are at work, you should avoid invading the personal space of other people. Give them some space.

Culture - What Makes Us All The Same While Still Making Us Unique

The fact that people come from a variety of cultural backgrounds makes it possible that some individuals will not understand the message that you believe you are conveying to them. It is very evident that the general public has no concept of what a scientific theory entails, and this is most likely the simplest illustration of the challenges that arise when one culture attempts to communicate with another.

A member of the public called us at 21:13 to advise that......," and I'm pretty sure you've seen and heard them say something similar no matter where you live (there's a reason that happens and it's called Role Theory, something I'll come back to later). So in my previous job, this was often an issue where the emergency services would want to say, "A member of the public called us at 21.13 to advise that......"

As a result, in addition to the national cultures that each of us has, there are also other cultures that may be found both within and outside of national borders. Because you have little understanding of these cultures, it will be difficult for you to formulate a message that would resonate with them. Without this information, it will be difficult for you to convey your message.

Bad Science is an excellent book that was written by Dr. Ben Goldacre, and if you haven't read it yet, I strongly suggest that you do so. In it, he discusses the media and how, via their coverage, the general public is led to have a misunderstanding of science. One of the challenges that arise when people from different cultures attempt to communicate with one another is shown by his assertion that journalists have degrees in the humanities rather than the sciences and "wear their ignorance as a badge of honor."

As someone who has a degree in both communications and the humanities, I can assure you that people of my culture take offense when they are labelled uneducated.

So let's assume I want to do research regarding street gangs by talking to members of those gangs for a study about how different gangs communicate with one another. Before I would talk to them, the first thing I would do is make an effort to find out a little bit more about them. Do I need to dress professionally and bring my notes with me in a briefcase if I want them to speak to me, or can I get away with wearing jeans?

However, if I want them to feel comfortable enough to share their thoughts and feelings with me, what kind of conversation should I have with them? I would imitate the rhythms of their speech without trying to be condescending by attempting to mimic it word for word. I would need them to realize that I am not all that dissimilar to them, but I would also need them to see that I am not one of them. It would be necessary for me to keep some distance from them while yet being near enough for them to welcome me into their subculture.

Or, how should I contact scientists who are involved in science communication in order to conduct an interview with them when they are attending a scicomm conference for my master's degree?

Given that this genuinely took place, a brief explanation is in need given the unexpected nature of the occurrence from an anthropological standpoint. Because I wanted to gain experience doing more in-depth research before applying for a PhD, I decided to pursue a Master of Arts degree instead of a Doctor of Philosophy degree. I choose Public Relations and Multimedia Communication as my area of study because it allowed me to concentrate on my thesis while also enabling me to coast to some extent based on my previous work experience. In point of fact, I came close to introducing myself to each participant in the same manner: "I was researching science communication; however, I was studying PR rather than science communication; therefore, it was an MA rather than an

MSc; however, I have worked in PR and communications for years."

Before I stated those final nine words, I was looked at with disdain by many people; I could practically see them thinking that this wasn't my area of expertise. The last nine words I uttered caused a shift in their perception of me; they began to see me as someone from whom they could get assistance on a much higher level, and about half of them approached me for my professional guidance. I also spoke to a few professional communicators who handle scientific communication for their organization at senior levels, and surprisingly enough, their response was the complete reverse of what I was expecting.

So, let me ask you this again: what was it that Ben Goldacre said? Even though it wasn't a part of the study project, the fact that you were interviewing people from their culture revealed a lot. It's probably a good thing that I don't consider the 25 out of 40 persons I questioned who admitted to doing that to be a trustworthy sample size (that's 62.5%, in case you're curious).

Anyway, let me go off topic. I would take into consideration their culture in order to ensure that meaningful dialogue can take place, which is necessary for making the Schramm model of communication work and producing useful feedback. Journalists use this tactic as well, which is why a person who can report on a conflict can also conduct interviews with prominent officials and street gangs. They modify their behavior to fit the customs of the individual with whom they are interacting.

When I was interviewing scientists at the British Science Museum during an evening event, I thought about how they would be dressed and matched this. However, wearing a NASA t-shirt was a mistake since the public believed I worked for them; I also adjusted my speech patterns to match those of the scientists I was interviewing. Even though I was conducting interviews for research, I did it in a journalistic manner, so it seemed more like a chat than an interrogation.

In point of fact, what I was doing was adapting my practices to fit theirs in order to encourage people to open up, and I was using the Schramm model by paying attention to the feedback in order to get the information I need.

When it is you interacting with them, the process is the same; first, you examine their culture, and then you change your message to match it. Finally, you use feedback to improve and adapt it to meet the cultural norms and understanding of the people you are communicating with.

The dynamic consists of them coming up with a message based on what they interpret as the expressions of the other participants.

The participants will be arranged in a circle and instructed to stand next to one another.

The leader of the group will stand in front of the first member, take the phone, and deliver a message to him or her in a low voice. The leader will then hand the phone to the participant who got the message, and the person who received the message will repeat the activity.

It is required of him or her to stand in front of the other member and, with the telephone in hand, repeat the message that the leader stated. If he or she cannot recall the message, then it is required of him or her to make one that is as similar as possible to the one that they heard.

In this manner, the person who is next in line will get the telephone along with a message before the last participant is reached.

In most cases, the last participant's contribution will result in a message that is distinct from the one that was sent by the person in charge of the discussion.

After that, they will be tasked with coming up with a new message that is at least somewhat analogous to the previous one, and they will have to piece it together using the foundational phrases that each individual has been exposed to.

The objective is to encourage the growth of thinking, and by extension, to foster thinking that is distinct from, and independent of, the patterns of daily life.

16 THE BOAT DIES IN THE WATER

Rope is one of the necessary components for this dynamic.

The bare minimum required is between 20 and 25 persons.

Approximately forty-five minutes will pass.

The purpose of the activity is to generate ideas that may assist the sinking ship in making it to shore in one piece.

After the participants have formed a large circle, they should use the rope to create another circle around themselves, and after everyone is contained inside the original circle, they should tie a knot to complete the activity.

Once the dynamic has begun, the leader has to make it very apparent to all of the members that they need to engage.

Everyone should start moving about within the circle as the leader walks among them and shouts out loud, "the ship is sinking, the ship is sinking, what shall we do?"

At that point, everyone pauses what they are doing, and someone raises their voice to provide a suggestion. For instance, someone can say, "let's look for the life jackets," after which everyone begins to act out the process of looking for the life jackets and putting them on.

The same dynamics govern the continuation of the exercise, and the leader keeps strolling among the participants while repeating, "the boat is sinking, the boat is sinking, what shall we do?"

They come to a halt once again, and one of the participants grabs the microphone, saying, "let's give each other a hug." Continue in this manner until all individuals, including the kid or teenager with Asperger's, have had the opportunity to contribute by providing their own suggestion to either salvage the boat or survive the circumstance.

In the last paragraph, a brief conclusion is drawn on the significance of continuing to generate and contribute our own thoughts, even during the most trying times.

How To Get Rid Of Your Obsessive Compulsive Disorder With Eye Contact Staring?

Even though there isn't a medication or therapy that's been approved for completely curing individuals of their OCD, there are strategies to lessen the impact of obsessive thoughts and prevent oneself from giving in to compulsive behaviors. Some of these methods include the following: avoiding situations that might trigger the obsessive thoughts.

Don't Hold Everything Inside of You.

Even while it seems to be the most secure location to be in or to hide, in reality, it is not. It's possible that talking to trustworthy friends and family members about what's going on can help reduce the attraction of those recurring ideas and pictures. Do not be afraid to seek the expert assistance of a psychiatrist who is trained in medicine. One of the most effective forms of self-help therapy for obsessive-compulsive disorder (OCD) is talking about your struggles with the condition to individuals in your life whom you can confide in and who are knowledgeable and experienced in matters relating to the condition. Joining a support group will allow you to hear other people with OCD discuss the issues they have dealing with the condition, and it will also provide you with a safe space in which you may bare your soul without the fear of being ridiculed. As you talk about the challenges you face on a daily basis with others who really get it in support groups, you'll also have the opportunity to assess how much you've grown and how much you've improved.

Alter Your Vacation Plans.

It is possible that the anxiousness may become rather unsettling. To such an extent that, in an effort to resist giving in to the compulsive routines, one can seek solace in alcohol, cigarettes, or other substances that are both unlawful and highly addictive. The majority of people who have this illness make this error in judgment all the time. The reality is that neither nicotine nor alcohol are effective in any way in calming the nerves. Stimulants are given this name because they induce the body to become more active and, as a consequence of this, more nervous. After the very temporary comfort brought on by these items, the invasive thoughts quickly make their way back, often becoming much more powerful than they were before. Looking to substances like alcohol and drugs as a kind of solace is really self-destructive since it simply serves to exacerbate the situation. Alter your means of escape.

Make Adjustments to Your Lifestyle.

The majority of individuals who are affected by OCD have their lives organized entirely around the condition itself. They make every move and decision in life with their OCD serving as the guiding principle, and they spend their lives completely at the whim of unwelcome thoughts. Determination will play a significant role in this, as it will in every therapy that is described here. You have the will and the desire to break free from the bonds that OCD has placed around you, and you are the one who will ultimately choose whether or not you will live a happy life. Especially if you have begun to feel as if you have lost control of your willpower as an independently determined person, increase the frequency with which you go out for a run. Increase the frequency of your workouts and keep your body in control. Be sure to eat in a way that is good for your body and at the right times. Spend time with your loved ones and friends, travel, and immerse yourself in the great outdoors. Try as much as you can to get a sufficient quantity of sleep every night. This last step may not be as simple as it seems, given that obsessive thoughts can make it difficult to fall asleep, which can lead to both sleeplessness and sadness. Once again, determination will be the thing that makes the difference.

Shift your attention elsewhere.

Finding out more about yourself can make accomplishing this goal much easier. What are some of your favorite activities to participate in? What are some of your natural gifts and skills? If you find that certain ideas keep popping into your head, you should actively work to redirect your attention. And certainly, you shouldn't simply sit there arguing those ideas and pictures in your head. They never lose an argument because they are so tenacious and never give up. Take action in the direction of those optimistic ideas. Instead of rushing for the easy solution (your compulsions), you should go towards a paintbrush. Put on your go-to program on television or cook yourself a delicious dinner and give yourself a break. It might even be as simple as picking up the phone and contacting someone or going out with a friend and having a good old-fashioned chat. Because it provides you with an alternative to condemning yourself and putting yourself down, this method of self-help is an effective therapy. You no longer have to feel guilty or ashamed because you will learn to appreciate the kindness and rich beauty that are intrinsic to you. You have arrived at the realization that, rather than worrying about whether or not others would accept you, you have found that they would probably be attracted to you if all you did was show them the vibrant beauty that exists inside your own heart and soul.

Other treatments that have received medical clearance include as follows:

Exposure and Response Therapy (also known as ERT)

Patients undergoing this kind of cognitive behavior therapy are urged to deliberately go in the direction of whatever it is that their brain is continuously advising them to avoid. They are advised to embrace the 'threat' rather than running away from the risk and behaving compulsively to alleviate the tension. This helps them avoid the obsessive behavior. This implies that if a person with OCD has an excessive fear of making eye contact, they may be instructed to look at another person in order to work through the anxiety that develops until it is diminished and the scenario no longer seems as dangerous. Some patients describe experiencing feelings of boredom over a period of time, when the ideas do not ring as often as they once did. The patient will begin to understand that they do not have to give in to those obsessive habits if this is done often enough and to the appropriate degree. It's almost like retraining the mind to accurately differentiate between circumstances that really pose a threat and those that don't.

Being mindful

This technique of cognitive behavior therapy is maybe the most vital social skill, but it is also one of the most undervalued. Patients are strongly urged to shift the way in which they are concentrating their attention. The practice of mindfulness involves directing one's attention on the person, the activity, and the conversation that are occurring in the present while relegating distracting thoughts and feelings to the status of meaningless background noise. This means that if a person with OCD has an obsessional fear of making eye contact, they are counseled to shift their attention to the conversation or to the person they are talking to rather than being overly conscious of themselves and acting compulsively to relieve the anxiety or to avoid the conversation they are engaged in. This is done in place of the person with OCD being overly conscious of themselves and acting compulsively to avoid the conversation they are engaged in. This not only makes it easier to participate more actively and organically in the discussion, but it also makes it easier for those who struggle with eye contact anxiety or OCD.

If you are feeling uncomfortable staring at the person you are speaking with, it is OK to look away for a little while.

I used to suffer from anxiety whenever I made direct eye contact, but ever since I discovered this strategy, my life has been drastically improved. Whenever I have a discussion with someone, I not only listen to what they have to say, but I also pay attention to how they say it, including whether they are happy or unhappy and how they carry themselves during the conversation. My attention switched from being very self-aware to naturally conversing with curiosity and self-assurance as a result of this, which dramatically transformed my emphasis.

Medical treatment

Clomipramine and other types of antidepressants, such as those used to treat depression, might be prescribed to OCD patients by licensed medical professionals on the basis that the condition often results in depression. Be sure to carry out the instructions to the letter, and do not stop taking the medication unless your doctor specifically tells you to. If this treatment does not have the desired effects, the physician may recommend trying a different kind of selective serotonin reuptake inhibitor. Inhibitors or selective serotonin reuptake inhibitors like fluvoxamine. Risperidone or other antipsychotic medication may be suggested later on if there is little to no improvement after the first treatment. They are known as "happy pills" due to the fact that they increase the amount of the neurotransmitter dopamine that is produced by the body while decreasing the amount of the neurotransmitter serotonin that is produced by the body. Serotonin is a neurotransmitter that is implicated in depression.

Don't Give Up!

Do not give up after your first unsuccessful try. Not everyone feels comfortable striking up a conversation with someone who is somewhat close by. People who can only respond to your inquiries with a single word or a single phrase may sometimes cross your path. If they do, don't be surprised if they are described as monosyllabic. Please don't take anything I say personally. It is not you; the problem is with them.

There are occasions when somebody could have arrived with the intention of socializing with a certain group of people, which might not have included you on their list of targets. Because of this, there is a potential that they may get distracted and look for opportunities to withdraw from the discussion whenever they have the opportunity.

You haven't done anything wrong, but they just aren't interested in what you have to say.

People might be having a poor day for a variety of reasons, and as a result, they might not want to speak to you or could lash out at you. Make amends for having caused them such annoyance, and then proceed. You have no idea what they are going through, and displaying anger and hurt will serve you neither here nor anywhere else. Instead, it will bring down your mood and make you irritable toward other people.

The art of making polite conversation is comparable to that of riding a horse. When you are flung off of the horse, you do not yell at it, beat it with a whip, or quit up totally. You brush yourself off, get back up on your feet, and go on to the next horse in the hopes of successfully riding it. You will be successful; all that is required is effort on your part.

Take a few slow, deep breaths, shut your eyes, and tell yourself, "I can do this." If you find that approaching individuals gives you the chills or causes you to hesitate, try these steps.

You are the only one who can assist you in helping yourself. If the method I just described doesn't work, you may also try the following:

Discover the reasons behind your lack of self-confidence. Make an effort to think about the causes, as well as ways that you may get around them.

Accept the fact that you have a poor opinion of yourself. The first step in recovery is coming to terms with it.

Discussing the issue with another person will assist you in coming to terms with it and accepting it. Saying something aloud has the effect of making it more real to you and makes it less difficult for you to accept it.

Consider all the wonderful things that have occurred in your life, and then ask yourself, "If I am not a good person, why did these wonderful things happen to me?" Be careful to keep in mind, however, the things that did not occur by chance but rather as a direct result of your efforts. As an example, being given a promotion.

Face your fears head on. Try anything that demands a grain of self-assurance on your part. You should not be concerned about failing; what matters is that you are making an effort.

Educate Staff About The Key Performance Indicators Of The Company.

Employees truly do want to know what all those reports and figures represent, even if they don't directly ask about it. Managers that take the time to educate their workers on the essential metrics of the company will see higher levels of both comprehension and output from their workforce as a direct result of their efforts. Keep in mind that the act of imparting one's knowledge increases one's strength.

crucial statistics are the fundamental connection to knowing the big picture; nevertheless, many managers prefer to discuss them only on a "need to know" basis or seek to keep them from coworkers entirely. This is because crucial numbers are the primary link to comprehending the large picture. On the other hand, restricting access to this "intelligence" to just the management level makes little sense. Before the information is distributed, there can be no multiplication of power. Begin with the fundamentals. The numbers are the business gauges that express outcomes and define success; they are more than just figures on paper. They reveal how well the firm is performing, point out areas that may need some development, and show workers how the actions they take in their day-to-day work effect the organization and the people who do business with it. Some people have referred to this method of disclosing the data as "Open Kimono Management," meaning that it reveals what is really occurring behind the curtain of perception.

One of the most prestigious hotel brands in the world is the Ritz-Carlton hotel chain. Customer satisfaction is more than simply a slogan at their hotels; rather, it is ingrained in their operational philosophy. The manner in which management at The Ritz-Carlton communicates with its staff members is one of the reasons why the hotel routinely receives great ratings from guests. The "Open Kimono" management strategy is something they actively practice.

At each and every Ritz-Carlton, the teams gather for 10 minutes before the start of each shift to discuss important information. Each employee gets a tiny package that contains the day's critical information, including a forecast hotel occupancy, a list of VIP visitors and their preferences, unique conference/meeting requirements, and a motivating concept that will guide them throughout the day. These meetings guarantee that everyone is aware of the crucial figures on a daily basis and that each employee is aware of how they contribute to the overall level of customer satisfaction.

The "numbers kimono" may help clear out any uncertainty and remove any unhelpful emotions that may be interfering with the decision-making process. Although there is a place and a time for emotions in business, they should not be relied on as a primary basis for decision making. Instead, one should focus on the facts. workers are better able to grasp why certain choices are made and accept them as reasonable when they have been instructed on the important signals of the company, even if they do not necessarily agree with every decision that is made. This is true even if workers do not necessarily agree with every decision that is made.

The exchange of information is the cornerstone of creating understanding, which serves as the basis for the acceptance and support of co-workers. It alters how individuals think about the task that they do. They are well aware of their roles and the reasons for their significance. The more effectively you explain "what" as well as "why," the more effectively your team will be able to achieve the goals that you have set for them.

According to what Peter Drucker has stated, every single person working for a company should be aware of the answers to the following two questions: "What is our business?" and "How is business?" That is some sound advise to follow.

Charmingly Cool Charismatic

A great conversationalist has all of the characteristics listed above, including the ability to know what to say, how to say it, and when to say it. However, there is one more component that must be added to the mix in order to become an expert in small conversation. Is there anything else that stands out to you about successful people?

They have a magnetic presence.

Especially when it comes to motivational speakers like Tony Robbins and Les Brown, they seem to have the power to captivate an audience while they are speaking. They have a way of capturing your attention from the time they start talking. This is an example of charisma in action. Others have to put in more effort in order to achieve the same level of attraction as those fortunate enough to have it naturally. It is a talent that can be acquired, despite the common misconception that it is an aspect of a person's personality.

To grow charisma, you're going to need time and practice, just as it takes time and effort to build confidence. However, if you persevere and stick at it, you're going to get there eventually. Before you can even begin to improve on your naturally endearing personality, you need to first:

Develop Your Command of the Foundations of Conversation

Before you can start working on your charisma, you need to focus on developing the foundations of your conversational abilities. To do this, you may use the strategies that were covered in the early chapters of this book. When people are charismatic, they appear to know just how to speak to people, how to start a conversation, how to keep it going, how to lead it in the direction they want, and how to demand people's attention with the things that they say. If you examine charismatic people attentively, you will notice that they seem to know precisely how to do all of these things. They are proficient in the fundamentals.

You need to put in some effort and practice initially in order to build your talents in making casual conversation. You shouldn't go to the next step of charisma growth unless you've reached a level of self-assurance in which you feel you can adequately represent those talents.

1. You have to get in the habit of smiling. Also, avoid making it seem forced. The grin of a charismatic person is one that is easy, natural, and at ease, as well as one that is warm, genuine, and welcoming. During your interactions with other people, the grin that you are projecting should look somewhat like this. When one person smiles at another, it immediately puts them in a better mood and helps them feel more at ease throughout the conversation. When you grin, you make yourself seem friendlier, and when you smile in a genuine way that lights up your face, the other person is more likely to smile back at you. One of the most important characteristics of a captivating person is a genuine grin that they always wear. Every day, stand in front of a mirror and practice smiling at yourself. As you do so, focus on achieving a calm and joyful state of

mind. Then, evaluate the results. Does it have a natural enough appearance? Do you get the impression that it is stiff or forced in any way? During a period of small chat, the most effective method for projecting a grin that is genuine is to desire to interact with the individual. It is no longer as if you are being coerced into doing anything even when you have a strong desire to engage in that activity.

2. Maintain an appropriate amount of eye contact at all times.
You should direct your gaze on the person with whom you are having a conversation, but you shouldn't stare them down in a way that suggests you are attempting to compete with or intimidate them. During a discussion, it is essential to make eye contact with the other person since doing so communicates to them that you are paying attention to what they have to

say, that you consider what they have to say important, and that you believe they deserve your attention. Have you ever been having a discussion with someone and noticed that they were preoccupied with something else or looked away from you when they should have been looking at you? It's so annoying that it borders on insulting at times! Holding a person's gaze for one second longer than you would normally is recommended as the optimal way to sustain eye contact for an extended period of time. When you practice making small chat, make it a point to maintain eye contact with the other person, hold their gaze for a little bit longer than usual, and then glance away from them momentarily without moving your head away when you blink. Putting this into practice in front of a mirror, when you meet people in the morning, with your coworkers at work, and with the cashier who is checking out your groceries are all great opportunities to hone your skills. There are a lot of practice chances available to you; all you have to do is start taking advantage of them so that you may grow better at what you're doing.

3. Don't Hold Your Breath

People that exude charisma are expressive with their body, but not to the point where it becomes distracting or excessive. They do not stand there throughout the chat seeming as rigid as a board with their arms held tightly by their sides. This is something that uneasy individuals do, and it's something you should make it a point to steer clear of. During a discussion, you need to maintain a calm demeanor and gesture with just the perfect amount of energy to convey your excitement, but not to the point where you are going over the top with it. Be conscious of your hand movements and facial expressions while you work on perfecting small chat in front of a mirror. Are you nodding quite an excessive amount? Are you wreaking havoc with your hands in an overly enthusiastic manner? These are the kinds of little actions that, from your perspective, don't appear to amount to much, but from someone else's perspective, they may mean something quite different. It's possible that some people won't like it, others will be turned off by it, and yet others may find it unpleasant to be in your presence. while you've had a chance to hone your skills by yourself in front of a mirror a few times, it's time to solicit the opinion of some of your close companions on how you come across while you're conversing. Are you engaging in an activity to an excessive degree? Are you not putting out sufficient effort? You should strive to get a variety of viewpoints and honest opinions; this will allow you to maintain track of the areas in which you need to continue to improve as well as the areas in which you are currently excelling. It is also beneficial to watch videos of motivational speakers and lectures given by successful persons in order to get a sense of how they achieve their goals and to attempt to model one's behavior after that of the successful.

4. Use your wit.

The ability to make other people laugh without seeming to be trying too hard is one of the finest attributes of a charming person, yet it's also one of the most difficult to achieve. As with everything else that a charming person does, the comedy simply seems to flow organically as part of the discussion, and like everything else that they do, it looks to be nearly easy. People are drawn to those who have the ability to make them laugh. The secret to developing greater charm is to become someone who can make other people laugh without seeming to be trying too hard. Only then will you succeed. You may learn to be charming and acquire a sense of humor by first learning how to laugh at yourself. Being charming and having a sense of humor are both skills that can be learned. If you are able to do that, it tells others that you are self-assured and comfortable enough in your own skin that you don't mind if other people join in and laugh right along with you. This is a sign of confidence. The first thing you need to do is have the ability to laugh at yourself without feeling self-conscious. You will then be able to learn how to attune yourself to what other people's senses of humor are like, which is something that often occurs after you have had multiple conversations with the same person. Determine the appropriate humor for your audience by observing their reactions to various jokes. For instance, if you are in the company of a group of individuals who are more sensitive or reserved by nature, it is best to first be alert and refrain from making jokes so that you do not run the danger of upsetting anybody. This will ensure that you do not hurt anyone's feelings. Do not make the mistake of trying too hard to be humorous or of feeling the need to elicit a chuckle at every opportunity. Pick your moments, and when the chance presents itself, make the most of it.

5. Make the person with whom you are conversing feel like a VIP.
To dominate the art of small talk, one must become so skilled at conversation that they are able to make the people with whom they are conversing feel

important, respected, and that their thoughts and ideas are of significance. It is really not that difficult to achieve; the first thing that is required of you is to show respect. You should regard everyone as an equal, and nobody should be considered superior or inferior to you in any way. Show the person you are speaking with respect, and demonstrate that you are interested in what they have to say as well as enthusiastic on hearing what they have to say. In order to encourage people to open up and express their ideas on various topics, you might ask them questions. When they are speaking, pay close attention to what they are saying and respond appropriately when it is acceptable to do so. This may include showing agreement by nodding your head or by providing quick interjections to demonstrate that you are paying attention. Depending on the flow of the discourse, your brief interjections may be anything like "I see" or "I agree with that."

And as a last piece of advice, keep in mind that being charismatic is not the same thing as being a people-pleaser. There is a big difference between the two. You want others to find you charming and like you, but at the same time, you don't want to be the kind of person who caves in to everyone's demands. People that are charismatic are self-assured, and they have the ability to win people's favor based on the merits of their own personalities. It is OK for someone not to like you given the fact that it is impossible to get along with everyone in this world.

Sharing Information Within The Community

In today's society, there is a growing movement toward educating kids who have special needs to live as independently as possible in the community... in the "real world." This new course of study introduces a plethora of additional obstacles that must be navigated above, below, around, or through. When it comes to assisting a student in the development of a functioning comprehensive communication system, one of the most hard components is likely to be the process of developing effective and efficient communication techniques that can be used for active involvement in the community.

Surprisingly, there is a large lot of philosophical divergence about the types of communication that should be taught in order to facilitate involvement in community activities. There are purist theories and there are also practical theories. Regardless of the worldview that one subscribes to, there are a number of things that need to be taken into consideration.

The first truth is that a student's success in contexts as familiar as his school and home may not translate well to situations in which he or she is surrounded by individuals with whom they are less acquainted.

Some of the required communication functions for being successful in the community include being able to comprehend signals and information, providing information to others, and making requests. Learning to analyze one's surroundings is just as important as learning how to express oneself.

For the sake of this conversation, the term "community" will refer to the locations that the kid frequents that are distinct from his home and school environments. Community may refer to the student's neighborhood, places of shopping and dining, the houses of other individuals, places of worship, medical facilities, travel, and any other places that the student may go.

The second truth is that individuals within the group will have quite different levels of both their personal communication skills and their capacity to tolerate communication breakdowns. It does not matter what abilities the learner already has; there is always going to be a variable for which they cannot readily be prepared.

The third truth is that the community is unpredictable and lacks structure; it is the antithesis of an environment that has been meticulously designed, such as an educational setting, or a setting that is regular and tidy, such as a family setting. Because there are so many different ways to exchange information, get instructions, and determine how to achieve one's objectives, even those who do not have communication disabilities regularly face difficulties. People who have trouble communicating frequently have to contend with challenges that seem to be insurmountable.

The aspirations that teachers and parents have for their students run the gamut from optimistic to pessimistic. It's possible that the adult expectations that an adult has for how a student should operate in the community don't represent the kid's true capability. Students are often given so much protection that they are not given the chance to acquire the level of independence they could if they were provided with appropriate training and supports that were deliberately constructed. In contrast, when a significant amount of effort has been put in to modify for kids, people are able to perceive progress; yet, they often fail to identify how much of that accomplishment is the product of their own adaptations and accommodations. This might lead to students having a skewed expectation of their level of performance in other contexts. A highly realistic approach is needed in order to get a student ready for engagement in the community where they will be living.

The purpose of this chapter is to give a framework for understanding how visual communication tactics might be applied to the student's life outside of the classroom and the home. It is not the intention of this piece to provide a comprehensive analysis of augmentative communication. In the course of this conversation, we won't go into all the philosophical nuances that are associated with communication training. Instead, the subject of visual aids will be expanded to include yet another setting that is significant to students as the main emphasis of this session. When considering the possibility of their becoming involved in the community, keep the following fundamental points that have been brought up in our conversation in mind:

Visual tools provide assistance at all stages of the communication cycle, including comprehending, organizing, and conveying ideas and information.

Everyone has access to a variety of visual aids within their surroundings. Everyone makes use of them.

There are times when the solutions to large problems lie in a multitude of seemingly little details.

Any of the suggestions presented in this book may be modified to cater to the requirements of the community.

GOALS FOR COMMUNITY PARTICIPATION TO BE SET UP FRONT AND CENTRAL

This section's emphasis will be on persons who have the capacity for autonomous or supervised performance in the community because, taking into consideration the current social and educational trend to encourage expanded community engagement for people who suffer impairments, the scope of this section will be to concentrate on such individuals. Even though students' level of communication skill is a major factor in how effectively they will achieve their community objectives, many students who struggle with severe communication problems are capable of achieving a high level of success in community settings with the help of appropriate training and assistance.

There are apparently a lot of different schools of thought on the best way to get pupils ready to be productive members of society.

Yes! One school of thought advocates the concept that the community ought to make a great deal of effort to meet the requirements of those who have unique requirements in their lives. The opposing attitude says that people who have special needs should acquire appropriate compensations in order to have successful interactions within the society. It is vital that we teach our pupils with a sensitivity that will allow them to appropriately operate in the circumstances they will live in, despite the fact that society is now struggling with this philosophical dilemma. In order to accomplish this goal, it is important to ask a few questions.

Which questions are you referring to?

Despite the fact that there are numerous, the following are the most important considerations to make.

QUESTION 1: What do the student's parents see for their child's future? This is an important point to consider. Otherwise, the time spent instructing a pupil may not be moving in the right direction toward the goal. Where is he going to call home? Where exactly will he be employed? Who will he hang out with when he has free time? Where does he intend to go? What kinds of obligations will be placed on his shoulders? The basis for targeting specific abilities for each individual student will begin to take shape after the questions posed here have been answered. The student's present age, skill level, the mentality of his family, and the culture of the community in which he lives will all have a significant impact on the philosophy that he adopts about education. It is essential to keep in mind that the responses may shift over time due to changes in factors such as the ideology of the family, the age of the student, and the kid's level of prospective talent or lack of skill.

The Three-Step Process That Is Necessary to Be Assertive

To become more forceful, you need to break out of your typical patterns of conduct. The Three-Step Approach, often known as the ABC Approach, is an excellent tool for assisting you in intentionally honing your assertiveness skills. The ABC strategy consists of the following three steps:

A- Initiating the occurrence of an event

B - Beliefs that you have about it C - The repercussions of it

Consequently, bearing the preceding chain of events in mind, the only aspect of a situation over which you have control is the manner in which you feel about it. It is not feasible for chance to have been involved in either the actual incidence or the cause. When attempting to include assertiveness, you must be honest about your views, but you must never allow your convictions to be transformed into negativity. Being honest about your beliefs is a must for incorporating assertiveness.

It is imperative that every one of your communications be transformed into impactful "I" messages. You are able to more readily establish your particular values and opinions as a result of this. Additionally, it demonstrates that you are able to take responsibility for the comments that you make. Making use of these I-statements has the most crucial purpose of making your speech factual and devoid of any myths or preconceptions that may have been there.

Making A Case For Yourself In The Working Environment

Many women have the mindset that the job is based on merit, meaning that if you do well, you will be paid for it. The reality is that putting forth solid effort is not the only requirement. If you want to advance in your career, you need to demonstrate that you have faith in your skills and talents. Being forceful is one approach to accomplish this goal.

Regrettably, women have a propensity to avoid engaging in the behaviors that would facilitate their professional advancement. Let's take a look at the four most common concerns associated with assertiveness that prevent women from realizing their full potential in the job.

Concerns about the use of a forceful tone of voice

Women tend to speak more gently than males. We choose to utilize language with less impact rather than words with more gravitas. When we speak, we often begin our statements with "I think" or "I feel." People who are assertive, on the other hand, do not qualify or soften the things that they say; rather, they state their opinions unequivocally and without any preface.

It is more common to say "This is a good idea" rather than "I think this is a good idea." In a same vein, "I believe that this is the appropriate action to take" might be rephrased as "This is what we need to do."

You would agree that the latter, more forceful examples have a great deal more conviction, wouldn't you?

As has been established, one's level of assertiveness ought to be modified according to the circumstances. The situation is exactly the same in the office. There will be occasions in which modifying the tone of what you say is not just appropriate but also required. You may, for instance, use this strategy when it is time to settle a dispute between parties. Statements that begin with "I think" or "I feel" may be most effective at this time. However, if you want the members of your team to see you as a leader and you are in a serious meeting with them, it is in your best interest to adopt a position that is more self-assured and confident. Be careful not to come off as condescending, nasty, or diminishing in tone since this does not give you license to behave in such a manner.

Fear of engaging in bargaining

There is a significant disparity in pay between men and women in the workforce. Women not only make much less than their male colleagues do, but we also have a tendency to charge less for our services. When you really do the arithmetic, it's very terrifying. A difference of $5,000 in your starting salary at your first job will result in a significant loss of $200,000 over the course of your working life.

Do you believe that there is nothing in life that may be more embarrassing than asking for a pay raise? It's almost as though we're hardwired to feel bad about asking for financial assistance. There's also the problem that we don't know how much we're worth, which leads to us accepting whatever they give us because we believe it's the best we can get or that we deserve. This situation has to be resolved.

It is time for women to start being truthful with themselves about their capabilities and the contributions they can make to an organization. Since we were required to get the same qualification as our male colleagues in order to be considered for a certain post, we should be entitled to comparable salary.

You have to come to terms with the fact that you are valuable to any organization and acquire the skills necessary to negotiate the wage you are due. There is no one else who can do this task for you.

When I was presented with the opportunity to serve as Vice President, I was aware that the salary would be inadequate. I didn't condemn the men who made the offer since I am aware that corporations are always looking for ways to do tasks at the lowest feasible cost. Instead, I prepared myself by gathering as much information as I reasonably could about relevant topics, such as current employee wages, staff retention rates, and the relative pay levels offered by competing businesses. After I had given them this information, they made me an offer that was 20% greater than the offer that they had first made, in addition to performance-based incentives and bonuses for staying with the company. Never before have I left a meeting with such a sense of accomplishment.

So, demand what you're really worth. In the event that you do not obtain it, the satisfaction of knowing that you stood up for yourself can help to alleviate some of the pain associated with the loss.

Be concerned about starting a fight.

According to Harvard Business Review (2013), women are superior than males when it comes to forming and keeping relationships. This is a talent that will serve you well throughout your life and is essential to your success while working in an office setting. Because of this, we don't want to advocate for ourselves in the workplace for fear of damaging our relationships with our colleagues. There is a worry that displaying aggressive conduct might make other people uncomfortable and could even bring about confrontation. People don't aware that there are positive ways to engage in conflict and that they should seek them out. Conflict may be instructive if approached with courteous language and by maintaining an impartial stance. As you gain more experience, you will see that it is absolutely possible to be aggressive without driving people away, provided that you do it in the appropriate way.

You must also bear in mind that the purpose of your time spent at work is not to create new acquaintances. It is excellent if you are able to develop deep relationships with the people you work with, but in the end, you are there to work and complete your responsibilities. You are responsible for striking a balance between being forceful and contributing to an environment at work that is peaceful.

Distaste for engaging in one's own promotion

Have you ever taken note of the males in your life and how they constantly brag about their accomplishments? They will always have something to boast about, no matter where you are or what you are doing. It does not matter whether you are standing around a cocktail table at a company gathering or waiting for the meat to cook at a neighborhood barbecue. One of the reasons males tend to go up the corporate ladder more quickly than women is because of this.

As I was saying before, putting in decent effort is not enough to be successful. People have a right to know who you are, what you're capable of, and what benefits they may get from working with you. You need to be able to market yourself to others around you; if they are unaware of your skills and accomplishments, there is no reason why they should provide you with a chance.

I keep a record of all of my achievements, and when the occasion calls for it, I don't hesitate to brag about them. I believe that when most people think of self-promotion, the image that comes to their mind is of someone boasting loudly and inappropriately about themselves in a setting where they are making others feel uncomfortable. Do not be concerned; I am not referring to that kind of self-promotion in this sentence. No one is going to approach you at an inopportune time or in the inappropriate environment and urge you to discuss your accomplishments.

In spite of this, there is nothing that should prevent you from discussing your achievements, ideas, and accomplishments with your superior when you are in a meeting with them to talk about your future in the firm. In a similar vein, networking gatherings are neither the place nor the occasion in which you should be modest about your capabilities, credentials, or experience.

Think about compiling a list of all of your accomplishments and going back over it at regular intervals. When you find yourself questioning your capabilities, it is helpful to remind yourself of the accomplishments you have achieved in the past. This will give you a boost of self-assurance.

When things start to go south in a relationship, it is often up to you to make things right again. The resolution of conflicts is not always seen as a desirable aspect of a project manager's responsibilities. However, it is a significant component.

Because disagreements are an inherent element of working on projects. There will be resistance to change on the part of stakeholders, various priorities on the part of sponsors, and a keen interest on the part of team members in the manner in which your project is carried out. In point of fact, I could make the case that conflict is a positive thing.

You won't acquire the greatest answers to the challenges that your project is designed to solve if you don't provide yourself with a creative challenge. If the people who are supposed to care about what you are doing don't care enough to dispute about it, then they probably won't care enough when you deliver it.

Conflict is not just unavoidable; rather, it is something to be actively sought for.

A Guide to the Management of Conflict

This is the second and last section of a two-part series. The fundamentals of conflict management were discussed in the preceding chapter. In this one, we'll concentrate on the actionable activities that you can do to improve the situation at hand. This is a brief overview.

If you have not yet read part 1, I urge you to do so as soon as possible. If you look at the header for this chapter and it says "practical steps," you could get the impression that the first portion is merely unsubstantiated speculation. This couldn't be farther from the truth if it tried. There is a wealth of sound and useful guidance waiting for you there.

But let's pretend that you've already read Part 1 of the story. Part 2 also has a lot of material that needs to be covered in depth. Now then, let us get started...

The Process of Managing Conflict in Steps

Complexity is inherent in conflict. And if you do find yourself in a fight, there are three aspects of the situation that need to be addressed:

The intimate component

It's vital to pay attention to how you're feeling. You will make a mistake if you fail to recognize their existence. Dealing with feelings such as anger, frustration, guilt, resentment, and pride are probably going to be part of the process.

The meat and potatoes of the disagreement

This is the area of concentration that may seem the most natural to the majority of project managers. On the other side, some individuals have a propensity to attempt to calm emotional states while avoiding addressing the current issue.

The procedure for reaching a resolution

If you are able to maintain your method in mind at all times, then you will have a guide. Believe in it. You can go a long way with a decent method and a lot of good intent, but there will be some rough patches along the road. Rebuilding connections and addressing the underlying causes of the dispute are both possible outcomes of an effective procedure.

In order to make things better, we are going to base our work on a conflict management approach that consists of seven steps.

First, make the conscious decision to participate in a constructive manner.

This is probably going to be the most difficult phase. When you are feeling sad, furious, and full of wounded pride, it might be difficult to make the decision to reach out to others and try for a resolution to the problem. However, keep in mind that you are in a position of leadership. Therefore, the obligation is with you.

The second step is to make contact.

Get in touch with the other individual and let them know that you're prepared to work toward resolving the problem. You may not be ready to give up your job just yet, but I strongly suggest that you apologize unequivocally for any inappropriate conduct that you have shown in the past. And it is unquestionably beneficial to communicate your remorse that the two of you have ended up in a quarrel.

Step 3: Acknowledge and respect the bravery that your resister is displaying.

Show that you comprehend the other person's issues, or at the very least, that they have them. Demonstrate that you understand their problems. Make it very obvious that you are prepared to invest the necessary time and effort to fully comprehend and investigate their problems.

It would be a courageous choice on their part to participate in the process of resolution if they did. They are prioritizing their rational thought processes above their current feelings. They have the same likelihood of losing face as you do, so don't worry about it. Therefore, it is important to express gratitude to them for taking the initiative to work with you to find a solution to the problem you both face.

Fourth step: try to see things from each other's perspectives.

You need to be able to see things from each other's perspectives. You won't be able to find a solution to this problem unless you start from the same common foundation of facts about the issue, your definitions of it, your emotional reactions to it, as well as your worries and your dreams. Collaborate without offering any criticism in order to include all of the important facts and emotions. In addition, be sure to differentiate between facts and views. Recognize the worth of each other's perspectives while also coming to an understanding that they must be evaluated in light of the facts.

How To Have Profitable And Enjoyable Conversations And Why You Should

All forms of important encounters might potentially benefit from adhering to a few general principles. There are also other components at play in these discussions, aspects that need to be explored since they represent problems or barriers that need to be overcome. Investigate this, since it is the first order of business. Later on, I'll get to the standards for improving social conversations when I can. The most important instrument that we make use of and are required to deploy in order to communicate with one another is language. If language were a faultless or transparent channel via which one person could see into the mind of another person, it would improve human contact to the degree that it would almost approach the level of telepathy that is possible between angels. The unfortunate reality is that language works in precisely the other way. It is a method of communication that is very ineffective because it is obscure, opaque, and replete with ambiguities and traps for misinterpretation.

It is almost difficult for any one of us to use key words in the same manner that the people with whom we communicate would interpret them, particularly in terms of the significance that the words have for us. Even when we make a concerted effort to draw attention to the significance we place on a keyword, our cautionary remark often goes unheard, and the response to our questions or statements from the person with whom we are conversing reveals that he or she has either not heard or has not paid attention. Even when we make a concerted effort to draw attention to the significance we place on a keyword.

Naturally, one may anticipate that participants in the conversation will use language in a variety of settings during the length of the conversation. Everyone strives to use language in a way that is distinctive to themselves. Although this can't be changed, something can be done about it. It is possible for us to make a note of and even record the several meanings that are associated with the use of the same phrase. Although this involves more attention and effort than the majority of people are willing to invest in order to make their conversations more communicative, it must be done since failure to do so makes it impossible to avoid misunderstandings and even disagreements that seem intractable.

There are two things that might assist us in overcoming the difficulties caused by the inadequate medium of language. The first is a comprehensive education that covers a wide range of topics and includes a deep dive into the liberal arts subjects of language, rhetoric, and logic. The other is a history of teaching and learning that is passed down from generation to generation, a basis in shared reading, and an understanding of a very small number of core ideas. These two things had widespread use among our ancestors, notably in the eighteenth and nineteenth centuries of the modern era. Both the deterioration of our educational system and the extensive specialization that has been the hallmark of the 20th century have been stolen from us.

Our ancestors had a more comprehensive education in the liberal arts, which included both the abilities of study and the arts of communication. Those who had access to a good education and, as a consequence, were well-rounded persons had a same literary past. This provided them with the ability to communicate with one another using a vocabulary that included not just words but also ideas. Because of this, they were members of the same intellectual community, with a history of ideas, references, and allusions that they both had in common with one another. Because of this, communication between the two of them became easier and more efficient.

A well-educated person in the twenty-first century is no longer considered to be a generalist! In a certain field or domain, he is recognized as a leading authority figure. There are a number of terminologies that are exclusive to a specialist's field of work and are not used by specialists in other fields. These terms are included in the specialist's language. People who are highly educated in the twenty first century, or maybe I should say those who have had all of the schooling that is available up to college and university, may emerge from their reading of literature with very little in common despite the fact that they have all read the same works. This leads to what Ortega y Gasset calls "the barbarism of specialization," which is the antithesis of civilizational culture.

When having impersonal serious discussions, the heat of emotion is a second component that has to be regulated; however, this is not the case when having heart-to-heart conversations when emotions are the major focus of discourse. When done effectively, managing and controlling one's emotions in order to accomplish the work at hand is essential. Although emotions play a part in the dialogue that aims to be persuasive in some practical sense, they are regulated and controlled for the sake of the activity.

Emotions, on the other hand, have no place in impersonal discussions, the objective of which is to build a better understanding and agreement on the resolution of purely intellectual matters. Emotions are irrelevant to this conversation.

When emotions are brought into a debate like this, it taints the conversation and turns it into an emotional war when it should have been a rational competition instead. As a result, they descend into battles between opposing preconceptions rather than exchanges that seek for a meeting of minds about ideas or genuinely disputable perspectives, where the matter may be handled by abducting facts and marshaling argumentation. This is because exchanges that aim for a meeting of minds concerning concepts or legitimately disputable viewpoints are more likely to result in conflicts.

Self-awareness is another quality that, when present, contributes to the development of intelligent conversation and, when absent, hinders and frustrates such development. To comprehend others, it is necessary to first have a firm grasp of one's own identity. At the absolute least, one need to be able to have a straightforward conversation with oneself. It is necessary to have clarity in the soliloquy in order to have clarity in the speech. People who are unable of having an intellectual conversation with themselves are not likely to be capable of having an intelligent conversation with other people.

Make your train of thought known to others.

Keep in mind that individuals who are introverted often need some time to consider what they are going to say before they actually say it. Verbalizing your thinking process is an effective strategy that enables you to keep your naturally introverted inclinations while still making progress toward adopting a more outgoing character. Try to communicate your thinking process to the people around you, rather than waiting to talk until you are certain that you have formed your ideas in precisely the way in which you wish they had been produced. For illustration's sake, let's imagine that you and two other individuals are having a conversation on the acting career of Meryl Streep. A statement was made by one of them indicating that they believe Meryl Streep's acting career was at its peak prior to the year 2000. After that, they will inquire, "What do you think?"

As an alternative to having a thought in your brain that goes something like, "well, she was pretty good in The Devil

Wears Prada, but not so good in Mama Mia," you could instead...But, on the other hand, Mama Mia was never a very good movie to begin with...Ricki and the Flash were not successful either...Why can't we simply admit it? Being a little bit spontaneous can often bring a little of spice to a discussion that would otherwise be considered a little bit dull. Obviously, this strategy is not recommending that you start talking to others as if you were verbalizing your own personal stream of consciousness, but being a little bit spontaneous may add a bit of excitement to an otherwise somewhat boring interaction. Who knows, if you were to say what you were thinking about Meryl Streep's finest movies, rather than curating the ideal answer, you may wind up pushing another person in the discussion to add something that ends up being really exciting and pleasant to debate. This would be the case if you said what you were thinking about Meryl Streep's best movies rather than crafting the right response. There aren't many individuals who take pleasure in idle chatter, but an introvert often finds this to be an extremely trying experience. They will feel more connected to you if you offer them a window into your thinking process, and you will feel more connected to the discussion as a whole if you do the same.

Make use of the individual's name.

When you are having a discussion with someone, using their name is an essential strategy to use if you want to give the impression that you are more outgoing than you really are. This is especially true if you are trying to conceal the fact that you are an introvert. The whole of a person's life is impacted by their name, regardless of whether or not they are consciously aware of this fact. Do you know that there have been studies that have indicated that persons whose names begin with an A or a B are more likely to have better grade point averages than those whose names begin with C or D? For instance, did you know that these studies have been done? This is simply one example of the many studies that have been carried out demonstrating that the significance of our names cannot be overstated. In addition to this, and more significantly for the purposes of this book, a name is your direct gateway into the feeling of identity that another person has. Because it demonstrates that you have remembered the other person's name, using their name in the course of a discussion might even be unconsciously taken as a complement in certain cases. This means that you are conveying to this individual the sentiment that he or she is someone who stands out in your mind.

www.ingramcontent.com/pod-product-compliance
Lightning Source LLC
Chambersburg PA
CBHW050419120526
44590CB00015B/2022